VOCAL SELECTIONS

WONDERFUL TOWN

T0040862

Music by
Leonard Bernstein®

Lyrics by
Betty Comden and Adolph Green

Book by
Joseph Fields and Jerome Chodorov

Wonderful Town
The New Broadway Cast Recording
is available from DRG Records
DRG-CD-12999

ISBN 978-0-634-07396-0

7777 W. Bluemound Rd. P.O. Box 13819 Milwaukee, WI 53213

For all works contained herein:
Unauthorized copying, arranging, adapting, recording or public performance is an infringement of copyright. Infringers are liable under the law.

Visit Hal Leonard Online at **www.halleonard.com**

The Name and Likeness of "Leonard Bernstein" are registered trademarks of Amberson Holdings LLC.
Used by permission.

WONDERFUL TOWN

CONTENTS

8 Ohio

16 One Hundred Easy Ways

22 What a Waste

34 A Little Bit in Love

40 Pass That Football

29 A Quiet Girl

48 My Darlin' Eileen

56 Swing

73 It's Love

80 The Wrong Note Rag

PREFACE

by Betty Comden & Adolph Green

A phone call from George Abbott always held promise of excitement. Late in 1952, I (Betty) got a phone call and it was George asking if we could write the lyrics for a show based on *My Sister Eileen* to star Rosalind Russell. I (Adolph) was in Paris and got a call from me (Betty) telling about it, which caused me (Adolph) to rush home at once. It seems they had a partial score they were unsure of. George asked if we could write a score in four weeks because after that they would lose Miss Russell to other commitments, and wanted to know what composer we could suggest. We thought of Leonard Bernstein, knowing he had just returned from his honeymoon with Felicia, and mentioned him dubiously to George. George said: "Go over and ask him right away!" We did, although we were very doubtful if Lenny would be interested. Among other things he had promised his mentor Serge Koussevitsky that after *On the Town* he would get down to serious business and never, never write another show. We had no sooner entered Lenny's apartment and were blurting out the facts about the show when the phone rang. It was George, never one to waste time, barking at us impatiently, "Well, is it yes or no?!!" To our surprise, with no hesitation Lenny said "Yes." He always liked deadlines, and four weeks to write a score was an irresistible challenge.

The play by Joseph Fields and Jerome Chodorov written in the 1940's had been based on stories by Ruth McKenney about two girls from Columbus, Ohio, who come to New York in the mid-30's to seek fame and fortune. We resisted all pressure to update it to the 50's, and knew we were on our way when Lenny exuberantly banged out on the piano the Eddie Duchin vamp, a characteristic musical sound of the 1930's. We were creatively on our way to Greenwich Village and adventure in the "Big City," and were able to complete the score in the prescribed four weeks.

This show celebrates New York as the magnet for young people from all fields of endeavour who, like Ruth and Eileen, still come here to fulfil their aspirations in this Wonderful Town.

from *The New York Musicals of Comden & Green*
© 1997 by Betty Comden & Adolph Green (Applause Theatre Books, New York).
Reprinted by permission

PLOT SYNOPSIS

ACT ONE

Wonderful Town is set largely in Greenwich Village, that agreeable maze that isn't what it used to be, and probably never was. The time is the summer of 1935, and a guide is showing tourists the sights on Christopher Street. Ruth and Eileen Sherwood appear, fresh off the train from Ohio, and are tricked into renting a dismal basement apartment. Between visits from the clientele of the former tenant (a lady of dim virtue) and the blasting beneath for a new subway, Ruth and Eileen spend a grisly night, and wish they had stayed behind in "Ohio." The next day, Eileen, a blonde knockout, finds herself surrounded by suitors almost immediately, as usual, while Ruth, a would-be writer, attractive but lacking in confidence, is ignored. Ruth explains her system for "One Hundred Easy Ways to Lose a Man."

Ruth takes her manuscripts to the offices of a magazine edited by Bob Baker. He bluntly tells her that her melodramatic pieces are bad, and that she should write about things she has experienced. He laments the waste of talent in New York ("What a Waste"). Later, feeling sorry for his gruffness with Ruth, he finds the apartment and meets Eileen, who at once falls "A Little Bit in Love" with him. Another visitor is the Wreck, a former athelete who is not exactly married to the girl who shares his lodgings. He is still dazzled by his college fame in football ("Pass That Football"), but does excellent ironing, and being unemployed makes himself helpful around the place. Ruth shows up and invites Baker for dinner, to which Eileen has invited Frank Lippencott, a drugstore manager who showers her with gifts from the daily specials.

As dinner time approaches, Eileen appears with still another guest, Chick Clark, a brash young newspaper-man who is hotly pursuing her. The five make a game try at finding mutual interest but the evening breaks up in an argument and Baker muses that what he really wants is "A Quiet Girl."

Determined to be alone with Eileen, Chick invents a newspaper assignment for Ruth, who dashes off to the Brooklyn Navy Yard to interview a group of Brazilian cadets. They, however, have nothing on their minds but learning the conga, and follow the distraught Ruth back to her apartment, dancing all the way. Once they meet Eileen, they switch allegiance immediately and near-riot ensues as they conga their way through the Village.

ACT TWO

Eileen is arrested for disturbing the peace, but so charms the police at the precinct that they are virtually her slaves, even after learning that she is not Irish ("My Darlin' Eileen"). Ruth manages to get Eileen released, and doggedly takes a job walking through the streets with a sign advertising the Village Vortex, a nightclub, where the new sensation "Swing" can be heard. Eileen realizes Ruth loves Baker and convinces him that without knowing it he is in love with Ruth. Baker exuberantly expresses his feelings in "It's Love." It now appears that Ruth's story about the Brazilian Navy has won her a job, and Eileen in turn has been given a chance to sing at the Village Vortex, thanks to the notoriety her arrest has brought. Together with Ruth, she sings an old family favorite ("The Wrong Note Rag"). At the club Baker and Ruth find each other. For Ruth and Eileen, New York has indeed turned out to be a Wonderful Town.

© 1999 by Betty Comden and Adolph Green

WONDERFUL TOWN FACTS

ORIGINAL PRODUCTION

Opened February 26, 1953 at the Winter Garden Theatre, New York
559 performances
Produced by Robert Fryer. Directed by George Abbott. Choreography by Donald Saddler. Orchestrations by Don Walker. Musical Direction and Vocal Arrangements by Lehman Engel. Scenic and Costume Design by Raoul Pène Du Bois. Lighting Design by Peggy Clark.

Opening Night Cast:

Ruth	Rosalind Russell
Eileen	Edith Adams
Robert Baker	George Gaynes
Chick Clark	Dort Clark
Wreck	Jordan Bentley
Frank Lippencott	Cris Alexander

Awards
New York Drama Critics Award: Best Musical

Tony Awards: Best Musical; Best Actress (Rosalind Russell); Best Choreographer; Best Conductor and Musical Director; Best Scenic Designer

2003 REVIVAL

Opened November 23, 2003 at the Al Hirschfeld Theatre, New York
Produced by Roger Berlind and Barry and Fran Weissler. Directed by Kathleen Marshall. Choreography by Kathleen Marshall. Orchestrations by Don Walker. Musical Direction and Vocal Arrangements by Rob Fisher. Scenic Design by John Lee Beatty. Costume Design by Martin Pakledinaz. Lighting Design by Peter Kaczorowski. Sound Design by Lew Mead.

Opening Night Cast:

Ruth Sherwood	Donna Murphy
Eileen Sherwood	Jennifer Westfeldt
Robert Baker	Gregg Edelman
Chick Clark	Michael McGrath
Wreck	Raymond Jaramillo McLeod
Frank Lippencott	Peter Benson

DISCOGRAPHY

Original 1953 Broadway Cast
Conductor: Lehman Engel
Principal Cast: Rosalind Russell, Edith Adams, George Gaynes
MCA 10050

1958 Television Cast
Conductor: Lehman Engel
Principal Cast: Rosalind Russell, Jacquelyn McKeever, Sydney Chaplin
Sony 48021

1986 London Cast
Conductor: David Steadman
Principal Cast: Maureen Lipman, Emily Morgan, Nicolas Colicos
Relativity 8260

1998 Studio Cast
Conductor: John Owen Edwards
Principal Cast: Karen Mason, Rebecca Luker, Ron Raines
Jay Records 1281

1999 Studio Cast
Conductor: Sir Simon Rattle
Principal Cast: Kim Criswell, Audra McDonald, Thomas Hampson
EMI Classics 56753

2003 Broadway Revival Cast
Conductor: Rob Fisher
Principal Cast: Donna Murphy, Jennifer Westfeldt, Gregg Edelman
DRG Records 12999

Ohio

(Duet)

Ruth and Eileen

Lyrics by
BETTY COMDEN
and ADOLPH GREEN

Music by
LEONARD BERNSTEIN

EILEEN: Oh, Ruth!

RUTH: Now, Eileen, everything's going to be all right.

EILEEN: It's awful!

mf

RUTH: Never mind, Eileen, try and sleep.

EILEEN: I *can't* sleep.

RUTH: Try, darling, make your mind a blank.

EILEEN: I did, but I keep thinking of Ohio.

Slowly (flowing)

D♭ G♭ D♭

EILEEN: *(plaintively)* *mp*

Why, oh why, oh why, oh,

RUTH: *mp*

8 lower, if possible

Why, oh why, oh why, oh,

mp

Copyright © 1953 by Amberson Holdings LLC, Betty Comden and Adolph Green
Copyright Renewed
Chappell & Co. and Leonard Bernstein Music Publishing Company LLC, Publishers
Copyright For All Countries All Rights Reserved

Gb
Why did I ev - er leave O - hi - o?
8 lower
Why did I ev - er leave O - hi - o?
Eb m
Db
Bb7/Db
Why did I wan - der to find what lies yon - der When
8 lower
Why did I wan - der to find what lies yon - der When
Eb
Eb7
Ab
Ab7
Fm
life was so co - zy at home?
8 lower
life was so co - zy at home?

D♭
G♭
D♭
Won - d'ring while I wan - der,
8 lower
Won - d'ring while I wan - der,
D♭7
G♭
why did I fly, Why did I roam,
loco
why did I fly, Why did I roam,
E♭m6
D♭
B♭7
Oh, why oh, why oh, Did I leave O - hi - o?
Oh, why oh, why oh, Did I leave O - hi - o?

E♭6
A♭7
D♭
B♭7
May - be I'd bet - ter go home.
May - be I'd bet - ter go O - H - I - O

E♭6
A♭7
D♭
G♭
E♭m
RUTH:
Now
May - be I'd bet - ter go home.
May - be I'd bet - ter go home.
pp

A la Shep Fields
F6
lis - ten, Ei - leen, O - hi - o was stif - ling. We just could - n't wait to get
mf

EILEEN:
out of the place, With Mom say-ing, "Ruth, what no date for this eve - ning? And

BOTH:
RUTH:
3
Pop with, "Ei - leen, do be home, dear, by ten." Ugh! The

EILEEN:
gos - sip - y neigh-bors And eve - ry - one yap - ping who's go - ing with who, And

RUTH:
EILEEN:
dat - ing those drips that I've known since I'm four. The Ki - wan - is Club Dance. On the

(EILEEN:)
bas - ket - ball floor.
What a bore! Jer-ry
RUTH:
Cous-in Maude with her lec - tures on sin. What a bore!
Black!
Ez - ra Nye!
Just hope-less!
Cous-in Min!
Han - nah Finn!
Bab-bit-ty!
Stuf - fy!
Thank heav - en we're free!
Pro - vin - cial!
Thank heav - en we're free!
fff
Explosion

D♭
EILEEN: (in crying voice)
G♭
D♭
Why, oh why, oh why, oh,
RUTH: (in crying voice)
Why, oh why, oh why, oh,
ff
G♭
Why did we ev - er leave O - hi - o?
Why did we ev - er leave O - hi - o?
D♭7
G♭6
Why did we fly,
Why did we roam,
Why did we fly,
Why did we roam,

E♭m6
D♭
B♭7
Oh why, oh why oh Did we leave O - hi - o?
Oh why, oh why oh Did we leave O - hi - o?
E♭6
A♭7
D♭
B♭7
E♭6
rall.
D♭/A♭
A♭7
May - be we'd bet-ter go home,
May - be we'd bet-ter go
May - be we'd bet-ter go O - H - I - O!
May - be we'd bet-ter go
rall.
D♭
a tempo
G♭
E♭m
D♭
home.
home.
a tempo

One Hundred Easy Ways

Ruth

Lyrics by
BETTY COMDEN
and ADOLPH GREEN

Music by
LEONARD BERNSTEIN

Copyright © 1953 by Amberson Holdings LLC, Betty Comden and Adolph Green
Copyright Renewed
Chappell & Co. and Leonard Bernstein Music Publishing Company LLC, Publishers
Copyright For All Countries All Rights Reserved

(Spoken flatly)
"Just get out, crawl under the car, tell him it's the gasket, and fix it in two seconds flat with a bobby pin."
A7
Dm
Fm6
bat your eyes and say, "What a ro - man - tic spot we're in."
G
G7
C
G7
That's a good way to lose a man. He takes you to the base-ball game, you
f
p
C
C6
G7
C
C7
sit knee to knee, He says, "The next man up at bat will bunt you'll see." Don't
Just say, "Bunt? Are you nuts?! With one out, and two men on base, and a left-handed batter coming up, he'll walk right into a triple play, just like it happened in the fifth game of the World Se-ries in 1923."
A7
Dm
Fm6
say, "Oooh, what's a bunt? This game's too hard for lit - tle me."

Faster (but light)
G
G7
C6
F7
That's a sure way to lose a man, A sure, sure, sure, sure
f
p
C6
F6
C6
way to lose a man, A splen-did way to lose a man. Just throw your
F6
G7
C
A tempo
knowl-edge in his face, He'll nev-er try for sec-ond base.
f
Eb G7
C
G7
C
Am
C
F
C
Nine-ty-eight ways to go, The third way to lose a man, The
mf
p
ff

G7
C
life - guard at the beach that all the girl - ies a - dore
Swims
p

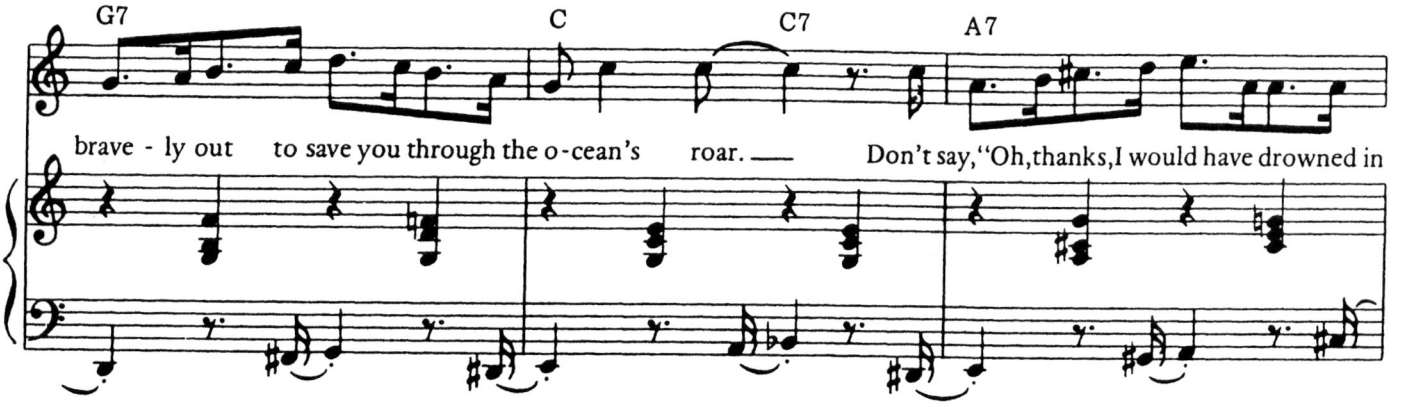
G7
C
C7
A7
brave - ly out to save you through the o-cean's roar.
Don't say, "Oh, thanks, I would have drowned in

Just push his head under water and yell, "Last one in is a rotten egg," and race him back to shore.
Dm
Fm6
G
G7
C
just one sec-ond more."
That's a swell way to lose a man.
You've
f

G7
C
found your per - fect mate and it's been love from the start,
He
p

G7
C
C7
A7
whis-pers, "You're the one to who I give my heart." Don't say, "I love you, too, my dear, let's
Just say, "I'm afraid you've made a grammatical error. It's not 'To *who* I give my heart', it's 'To *whom* I give my heart.' - - - You see, with the use of the preposition 'to,' 'who' becomes the indirect object, making the use of 'whom imperative; which I can easily show you by drawing,
Dm
Fm6
G
G7
C
a simple chart."
nev - er, nev-er part,"
That's a fine way to lose a man.
A
f
p
Faster
F7
C6
F6
fine, fine, fine, fine way to lose a man, A dan - dy way to lose a
Slow and free
C
F6
man.
Just be more well in - formed than he, You'll nev - er
p

G7
C
F6
hear "Oh, Prom - ise Me." Just show him where his gram - mar errs, Then mark your
G7
Am
With a beat
f
F6
tow - els "Hers" and "Hers." Yes, girls, you, too, can lose your man if you will
G7
A7
G7
use Ruth Sher-wood's plan: One Hun - dred Eas - y Ways To
D7
Db7
C6
C7
Dm
Ab7
C6
Db7
C
Lose A Man.

What a Waste

Ruth, Baker, and Editors

Lyrics by
BETTY COMDEN
and ADOLPH GREEN

Music by
LEONARD BERNSTEIN

Copyright © 1953 by Amberson Holdings LLC, Betty Comden and Adolph Green
Copyright Renewed
Chappell & Co. and Leonard Bernstein Music Publishing Company LLC, Publishers
Copyright For All Countries All Rights Reserved

G♯m
stars in their eyes. They're gon - na
F♯9
F♯maj9
con-quer the cit - y, They're gon - na grab off the Pu - lit - zer
Prize, But it's a ter - ri - ble pit - y
D/E
D♯m/E
Be - cause they're in for a bit - ter sur - prise.

E/D♯
N.C.
And their sto - ries all fol - low one line,
fp
f
(pointing to First Editor)
(pointing to Second Editor)
(pointing to himself with both hands)
Bouncy (𝅗𝅥 = 84)
E/D♯
G♯7
D♭
Like his, Like his, Like mine!
sfz
sfz
f
A♭/G♭
D♭/A♭
D♭
1. (Baker) Born in Du - luth,
2. (First Editor) Man from De - troit,
dim.
p
G♭
D♭/F
G♭
D♭/F
E♭m7
A♭7
Nat - u - ral writ - er, Pub-lished at sev - en– gen - i - us type.
Won - der - ful art - ist, Went to Pi - cas - so– Pab - lo said, "Wow!"

Db
Gb
Db/F
Gb
Db/F
Wrote the school play,
Wrote the school pa - per,
Sum - ma cum laud - e-
Set - tled in France,
Bought him a be - ret,
Lived in Mont-mar - tre,
F#m6
B7
E
E/G#
A
E/G#
all of that tripe.
Came to New York,
Got on the staff here,
Real - ly learned how.
Came to New York,
had an ex - hib - it,
sfz
A
E/G#
Ab7/Eb
Ab7
Db
This was my chance to be heard.
Well, since then I have - n't writ -
Art crit - ics made a big fuss.
Now he paints those tooth - paste ads
(p)
Db7
Gb6
Db6
- ten a word.
on the bus!
What a waste,
What a waste,
What a

A♭7/E♭ A♭7 D♭ D
waste of mon - ey and time!
mf
A/G D/A D G D/F♯
3. (Second Edtor) Girl from Mo - bile, Ver - sa - tile ac - tress,
4. (Baker) Kid from Cape Cod, Fish - er - man's fam - 'ly,
dim.
p
G D/F♯ Em7 A7 D
Trag - ic or com - ic, An - y old play. Suf - fered and starved,
Mar - vel - ous sing - er– Big bar - i - tone. Rent - ed his boat,
G D/F♯ G D/F♯ Gm6 C7
Met Stan - i - slav - sky. He said the world would cheer her some - day.
Paid for his les - sons, Starved for his stud - ies, Down to the bone.
sfz

F
B♭
F/A
B♭
F/A
Came to New York, Rep - er - toire read - y, Che - khov's and Shake - speare's and
Came to New York, Aimed at the op - 'ra, Sing "Rig - o - let - to" his
1
A7/E
A7
D
D7
G6
Wilde's. Now they watch her flip - ping flap - jacks at Childs'. What a waste, What a
(p)
D6
A7/E
A7
D
waste, What a waste of mon - ey and time!
2
A7/E
A7
D
D7
wish. At the Ful - ton Mar - ket now he yells "Fish!"
(p)
mf

G
D
A7/E
A7
"Fish!"
ad lib.
(in tempo)
ad lib.
(in tempo)
D/C♯
N.C.
Go home! Go west!
Go back where you came from!
in tempo
in tempo
fp
fp
Fast (♩ = 176)
D
Go home!
fp
f
fp
ff

A Quiet Girl*

Baker and Men's Chorus

Lyrics by
BETTY COMDEN and ADOLPH GREEN

Music by
LEONARD BERNSTEIN

* Original key was a minor third lower.

Copyright © 1953 by Amberson Holdings LLC, Betty Comden and Adolph Green
Copyright Renewed
Chappell & Co. and Leonard Bernstein Music Publishing Company LLC, Publishers
Copyright For All Countries All Rights Reserved

Andante (♩=60)
(suddenly calm)
p
Eb · Eb6 Eb Eb Eb6 Eb
An-oth-er kind, a dif-f'rent kind of girl?
sub. pp
Eb Eb6 Eb Eb6
(very slowly and tenderly)
p
Eb Eb6 Eb Eb6 Eb Bb F7/C
I love a qui-et girl, I love a gen-tle girl, Warm as
Bb/D F7 Bb Eb Eb6 Eb Eb6 Eb Eb6
sun-light, Soft, soft as snow. Her smile, a ten-der smile,
Eb Eb6 Eb Bb F7/C Bb/D F7 Bb
Her voice, a vel-vet voice, Sweet as mu-sic, Soft, soft as snow.

More flowing
mp
Gsus
Fm7
Gsus
Fm
D7/F♯
cresc.
When she is near me the world's in re - pose. We need no
mp
Gm
mf
Fm7
B♭7 rit.
p
E♭
E♭6
E♭
a tempo
E♭6
E♭
E♭6
words: She sees, she knows. But where is my qui-et girl?
mf
rit.
p
a tempo
E♭
E♭6
E♭
cresc.
B♭
f
F7/C
B♭/D
dim.
Where is my gen-tle girl? Where is the spe-cial girl, Who is
cresc.
f
dim.
F7
B♭
pp
F7/C
B♭/D
F7
B♭
soft, soft as snow? Some-where, some-where, my qui - et girl.
pp

E♭ E♭6 E♭
MEN'S CHORUS:
p (Humming in unison)
E♭6 E♭ E♭6 E♭ E♭6 E♭
B♭
F7/C
Humming
pp
B♭/D
F7
B♭
More flowing
BAKER: mp
Gsus
Fm7
Solo
Cho.
When she is near me the
mp
Gsus
Fm7
D7/F♯
cresc.
Gm
mf
Fm7
dim.
rit.
world's in re - pose.
We need no words:
She sees,
She
cresc.
dim. molto e rit.

Tempo I
B♭7
pp
E♭ E♭6 E♭
E♭6 E♭ E♭6
E♭ E♭6 E♭
B♭/D B♭
knows. But where is my qui-et girl? Where is my gen-tle girl?
pp
F7
cresc.
B7/D
p
F7/C
B♭
Where is the spe-cial girl, Who is soft, soft as snow?
cresc.
p
F7/C
pp
B♭
F7
rall. al fine
B♭ B♭6 B♭
B♭6 B♭ E♭/B♭
B♭
Some-where, some-where, my qui - et girl.
pp
rall. al fine
pp
dolce

A Little Bit in Love

Eileen

Lyrics by
BETTY COMDEN
and ADOLPH GREEN

Music by
LEONARD BERNSTEIN

Copyright © 1953 by Amberson Holdings LLC, Betty Comden and Adolph Green
Copyright Renewed
Chappell & Co. and Leonard Bernstein Music Publishing Company LLC, Publishers
Copyright For All Countries All Rights Reserved

F6
Dm
B7(6)
B7
haps a lit - tle bit more.
(rhythmically)
p
E6
B7
When he looks at me ev - 'ry-thing's ha - zy and all out of fo - cus.
sub.p
E6
B7
When he touch - es me I'm in the spell of a strange ho - cus po - cus.
A
F♯m7
It's so I don't know, I'm so I don't know, I don't

Am(maj7) Am6
cresc.
Bm7 Bm6
C aug. Am
C7
F6
Dm
know, but I know if it's love, then it's love - ly! Mm, It's so
cresc.
p sub.
Gm7
C7
F6
Dm
nice to be a - live When you meet some - one who be -
Gm7
A7
Dm
F aug.
witch - es you. Will he be my all, or did
F6
Gm7 B♭m6
F
Gm7
C7
I just fall a lit - tle bit, a lit - tle bit in

F6
Dm
Gm7
C7
love.
p, espr.
legato
F6
Dm
Gm7
C7
F6
Dm
Gm7
C7
Mm,
F6
Dm
B7(6)
B7

E6
B7
p
When he looks at me ev - 'ry-thing's ha - zy and all out of fo - cus.
p sub.
E6
B7
When he touch-es me I'm in the spell of a strange ho - cus po - cus.
A
F#m7
It's so I don't know, I'm so I don't know, I don't
Am(maj7) Am6 Bm7 Bm6 C aug. Am C7
know, but I know if it's love, then it's love - ly!

F6
sub.
p
Dm
Gm7
C7
Mm, It's so nice to be a - live When you
p
F6
Dm
Gm7
A7
meet some - one who be - witch-es you. Will he
Dm
F aug.
F6
Gm7
B♭m6
F
freely
in tempo
be my all, or did I just fall a lit-tle bit, a
freely
in tempo
Gm7
C7
F6
Fmaj7
lit - tle bit in love.
pp

Pass That Football

Wreck

Copyright © 1953 by Amberson Holdings LLC, Betty Comden and Adolph Green
Copyright Renewed
Chappell & Co. and Leonard Bernstein Music Publishing Company LLC, Publishers
Copyright For All Countries All Rights Reserved

(Cheering) Ray Wreck rah
Rah Wreck ray
Rah Wreck
Wreck Rah
Rah Wreck Wreck
W-e-c, R-e-k, R-e-q
Wreck, we love you!

Gb Gb/Bb Cb Gb/Bb Cb *poco rall.* Gb/Bb Bb7

Day that I left, Ev - 'ry-one gath - ered. Their cheer-ing still rings in my ears.

cresc. *f*

Same tempo (in 4)

D A7 D

'Cause I could pass a foot-ball Like noth - in' you have ev - er seen!

sfz *p* *f*

A7 D A7 D F#m

Could-n't spell a lick,

p

D6 B7 E7 E7/B A7

Could-n't do a-rith-me-tic. One and one made three, Thought that dog was c - a - t.

D6
A7
D
But I could pass a foot-ball
Like noth - ing you have ev - er seen.
f
sfz
p
f
A7
D
F♯m
D6
B7
Could-n't write my name,
Could-n't trans-late "Je vous aime."
p
E7
A7
D6
A7
Nev - er learned to read
Moth - er Goose or An-dré Gide.
But I could pass a
f
D
A7
C♯7
foot-ball
Like noth - ing you have ev - er seen.
sfz
p
f

F♯
C♯7
F♯
Could - n't fig - ure rid-dles,
Puz-zles made me pout,
Where the hell was Mos-es when the
p subito
C♯7
F♯
B7
lights went out?
I could - n't e - ven tell red from green,
p
p
E
A7
D
G7
Get those verbs through my bean,
But I was bud - dies with the Dean,
Like
pp
E7
A7
D
F♯m
noth - ing you have ev - er seen.
Passed with-out a fuss
f
ff

D6
B7
E7
A7
Eng - lish Lit and Cal-cu-lus,
Nev - er had to cram,
E - ven passed the bar ex-am,
D6
A7
D
Be-cause I passed that foot-ball
Like noth - ing you have ev - er seen.
f
sfz
p
f
A7
D
A7
ff
D
F#m
D
B7
Could - n't dance for beans,
Mashed my girls to smith - er - eens,

E7
A7
Some - times blood was spilled,
Still my card was al - ways filled.
D6
A7
D
'Cause I could pass a foot-ball
Like noth - ing you have ev - er seen.
f
sfz
p
f
A7
D
F#m
D
B7
Then there was the week
Al - bert Ein-stein came to speak.
E7
A7
Rel - a tiv - i - ty.
Guess who in - tro-duced him? Me!

D6
A7
D
'Cause I could pass a foot-ball Like noth - ing you have ev - er seen.
f
sfz
p
A7
C#7
F#
C#7
Had no ta - ble man-ners, Used ta dunk my roll,
p subito
F#
C#7
F#
B7
Al - ways drunk the wa - ter from the fin - ger bowl. Though I would not get up for an - y she, The
p
E
A7
D
G7
f
Prex - y's mom, age nine - ty-three, Got up and gave her seat to me Like
pp

E7
A
A7
D
D6
D
noth - ing you did ev - er see.
In our hall of fame
ff
p
B7
E7
A7
There's a stat -ue with my name,
There we stand, by heck,
Lin-coln, Wash-ing-ton and Wreck.
p
D6
A7
D
A
'Cause I could pass that foot - ball
Like noth - ing, you have
sfz
A
D
ff
ev - er, ev - er
seen.
ff
sffz

My Darlin' Eileen

(Based on an Irish Reel)

Policemen and Eileen

Lyrics by
BETTY COMDEN and ADOLPH GREEN

Music by
LEONARD BERNSTEIN

Copyright © 1953 by Amberson Holdings LLC, Betty Comden and Adolph Green
Copyright Renewed
Chappell & Co. and Leonard Bernstein Music Publishing Company LLC, Publishers
Copyright For All Countries All Rights Reserved

B♭
E♭
B♭
Take it from me, The May - or of Shan-non Would shoot off a can-non And
(Humming)
(Humming)

F7
B♭
ALL:
Gm
crown ye the queen. Dar - lin' Ei - leen, Dar - lin' Ei - leen!
Dar - lin' Ei - leen, Dar - lin' Ei - leen!
Dar - lin' Ei - leen, Dar - lin' Ei - leen!

Dm
Gm
C7
F7
f
B♭
Gm
Fair - est col - leen That i - ver I've seen. And it's Oh, I
mf
Fair - est col - leen That i - ver I've seen. Oh, I
mf
Fair - est col - leen That i - ver I've seen. Oh, I
mf
E♭
B♭
pp
F7
rall.
wish I were back in the land of the green with my dar - lin' Ei -
pp
rall.
wish I were back in the land of the green, dar - lin' Ei -
pp
rall.
wish I were back in the land of the green, dar - lin' Ei -
rall.
dim.
pp

Poco più mosso
B♭
E♭
leen!
leen!
leen!
SOLO (Ten. II)
mf
There's
SOLO (Bar. I)
mf (warmly)
I've seen them all: There's Brid - get and Shei - la,
Poco più mosso
mf
B♭
F7
B♭
Kate and De - li - lah and Moll and Mau - reen.
mf SOLO (Bar. II)
I've seen them all: Not
E♭
SOLO (Ten. I)
mf
B♭
F7
B♭
Or share the same street with My dar - lin' Ei - leen!
one can com - pete with,
ten.

TUTTI
f
Gm
Dm
Gm
Cm
F
Dar - lin' Ei - leen! Dar - lin' Ei - leen! Fair-est col - leen That i - ver I've seen, And it's
Dar - lin' Ei - leen! Dar - lin' Ei - leen! Fair-est col - leen That i - ver I've seen. And it's
mf
B♭
accel.
E♭6
molto
B♭
F7
B♭
Oh, I wish I were back In the land of the green With my dar - lin' Ei - leen!
Oh, I wish I were back In the land of the green With my dar - lin' Ei - leen!
accel.
molto
R. H. gliss
Dance
Allegro (like a Reel)
gliss.
f
1.
2.

f marc.

1.
2.
ff

C
EILEEN: (slowly, as before)
p
Dm7/C
C
Lis - ten, my lads, I've some - thin' to tell you I hope won't im - pel ye to
p

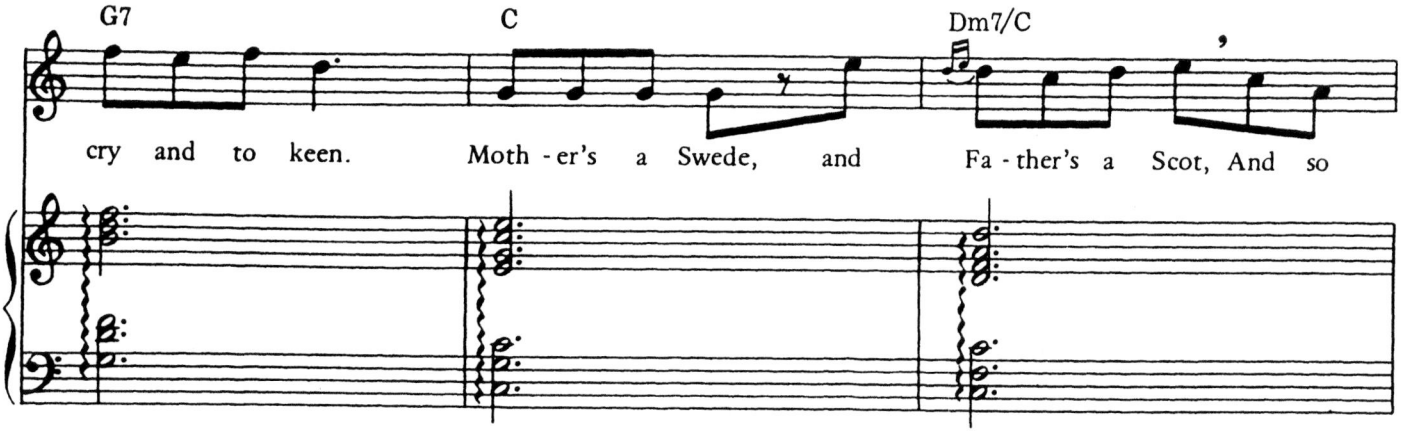
G7
C
Dm7/C
cry and to keen. Moth - er's a Swede, and Fa - ther's a Scot, And so

C/G
G7
C
Allegro, come prima
F
I - rish I'm not, And I nev - er have been!
Tenor (sounds as written)
MEN'S CHORUS:
f
Hush you, Ei - leen! Hush you, Ei - leen!
Bass
f
Hush you Ei - leen! Hush you Ei - leen!
Allegro, come prima
mf
Em
Am
Dm
G
Slowly again
C
Am
Fair - est col - leen That iv - er I've seen! Don't you hand us
Fair - est col - leen That iv - er I've seen! Don't you hand us
Slowly again
F6
F
C
ff
Allegro
G7
C
none o' that blar - ney! You come from Kil - lar - ney, You're I - rish, Ei - leen!
ff
none o' that blar - ney! You come from Kil - lar - ney, You're I - rish, Ei - leen!
Allegro
cresc.
R. H. gliss.

Dance
As before
f
1.
2.
f
ff
1.
2.
Tutti, shouting:
Ei - leen!
dim.
molto
ff

Swing

Ruth and Villagers

Lyrics by
BETTY COMDEN
and ADOLPH GREEN

Music by
LEONARD BERNSTEIN

Copyright © 1953 by Amberson Holdings LLC, Betty Comden and Adolph Green
Copyright Renewed
Chappell & Co. and Leonard Bernstein Music Publishing Company LLC, Publishers
Copyright For All Countries All Rights Reserved

VILLAGER: Hey, cats, get a load of that square!
Kra - zy Kats!
[Speedy V. on clarinet]
f
With bounce
Am C aug/G# Am C aug/G# Am C aug/G#
mf
Swing! Dig the rhy - thm! Swing! Dig the
mf
p
Am7/G♮ Am6/F# C Am C#dim7 G7
mes - sage! The jive is jump - in'and the mu - sic goes 'round and a - round Whoa - ho!
VILLAGER: Dig her!
Emaj7 B6 C#m7 E6 Am C aug/G# Am C aug/G#
Goes a-round and a-round. Cats, make it sol - id!

Am
C aug/G♯
Am7/G♮
Am6/F♯
C
Am
C♯dim7
Cats, make it groov - y! You got - ta get your sea - food, Ma - ma, your
G7
Em
Emaj7
B6
C♯m7
E6
fa - vor-ite dish is fish, It's your fa - vor-ite dish.
p
F7♭5
Don't be square, Rock right out of that rock - in' chair;
p
cresc.
f
E7
Truck on down and let down your hair, Breathe that bar - rel-house air!
cresc.
f

Am
mf
C aug/G♯
Am
C aug/G♯
The Vil - lage Vor - tex! Swing! Dig the rhy - thm!
mf
Am
C aug/G♯
Am7/G♮
Am6/F♯
C
Am
C♯dim7
Swing! Dig the mes - sage! The jive is jump - in' an' the mu - sic goes
G7
E♭ cresc.
E♭6
Edim7
C
'round and a - round, Get full of foo - ry - a - ky - sa - ky, Get
cresc.
RUTH:
B♭7
B♭9
f
E♭6
A♭9
G7
full of the sound of swing, The sol - id, jiv - y, groov - y sound of swing!
CHORUS:
(not square)
f
Swing!
f

Am/C E7/B Am6 C aug/G# Am C aug/G# Am7/G♮ Am6/F#
Dig the rhy - thm! Swing! Dig the mes - sage! The jive is
C Am C#dim7 G7 Emaj7 B6
jump - in' an' the mu - sic goes 'round and a - round Whoa - ho!
C#m7 (getting the idea) E6 Am C aug/G# Am C aug/G#
Oh!
Cat, make it sol - id!

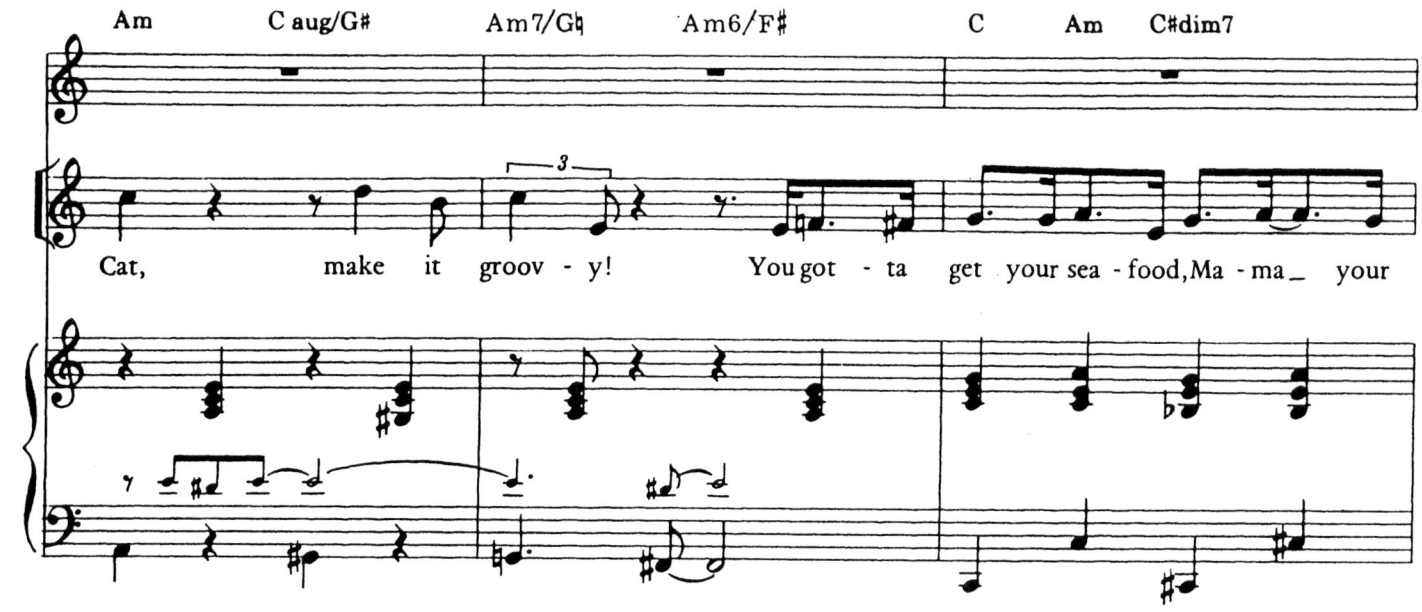
Am
C aug/G#
Am7/G♮
Am6/F#
C
Am
C#dim7
Cat, make it groov - y! You got - ta get your sea - food, Ma - ma_ your

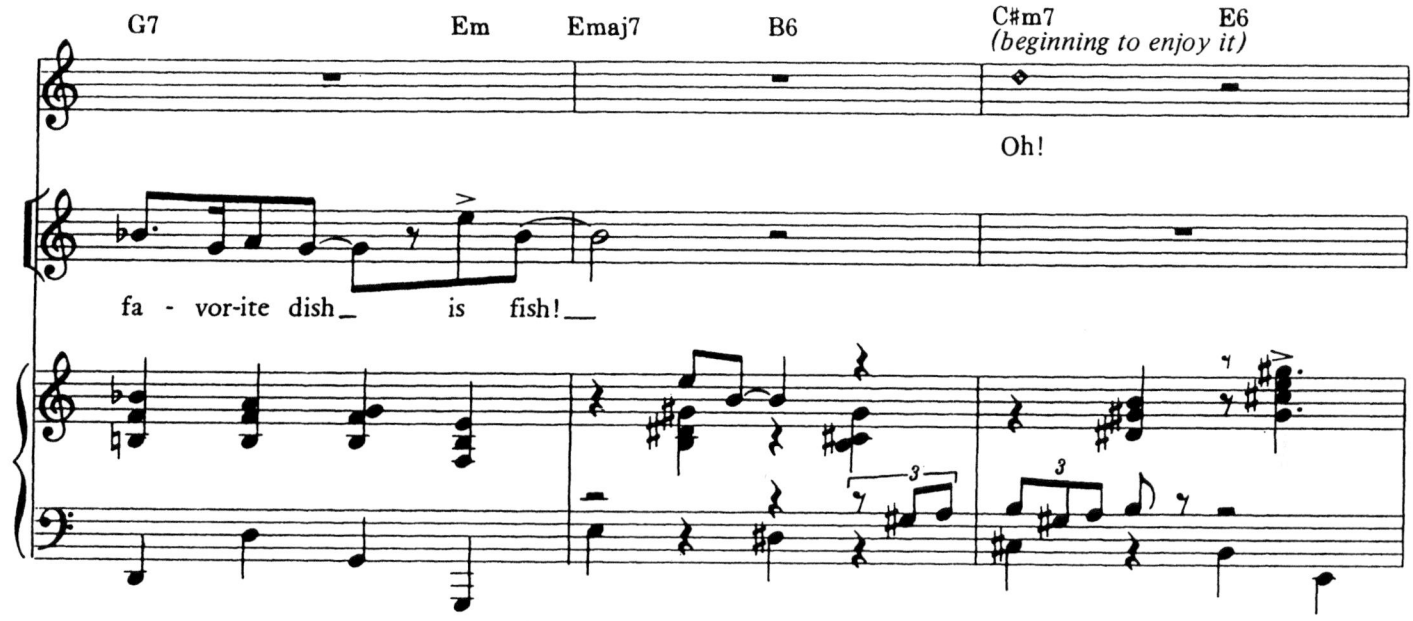
G7
Em
Emaj7
B6
C#m7
E6
(beginning to enjoy it)
Oh!
fa - vor-ite dish_ is fish!__

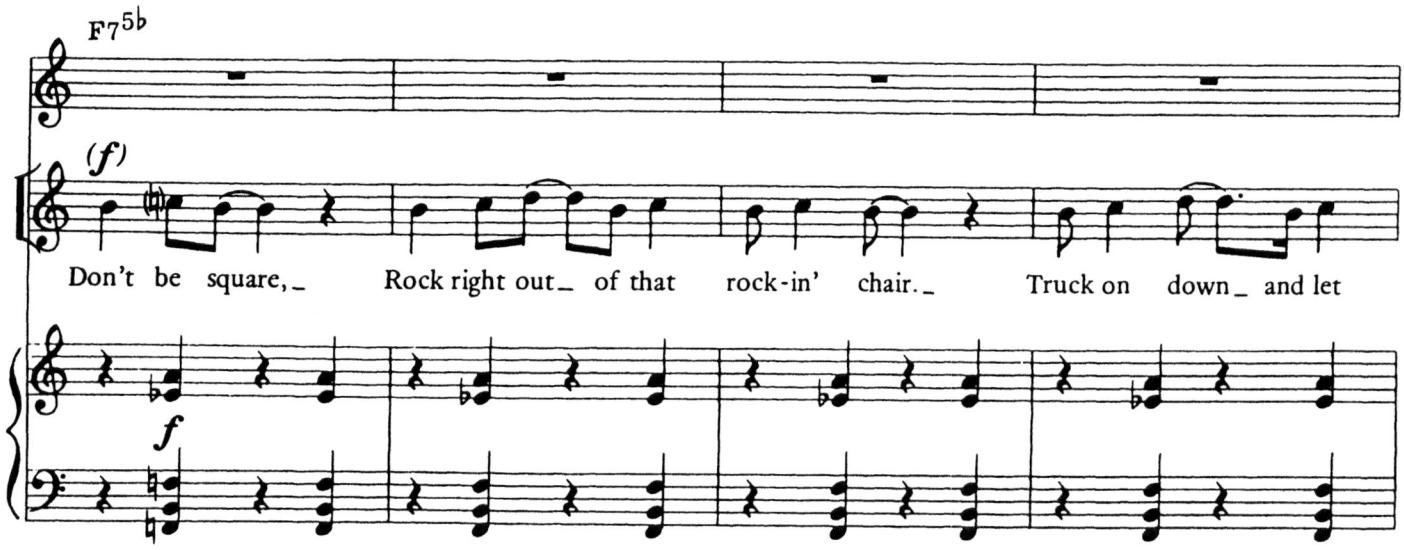
F7♭5
(f)
Don't be square,_ Rock right out_ of that rock-in' chair._ Truck on down_ and let
f

E7
down your hair; Breathe that bar - rel-house air!
You got - ta get with the Whoa -
f
ff
Whoa-ho - de - ho!
The
- ho - de - ho
The gut - gut - buck - et!
D9
gut - gut - buck - et!
Skid-dle-ee-oh day!
Skid-dle-ee-oh day!

A6
pp
Hee - dle, hee - dle, hee - dle!
pp
Hee - dle, hee - dle, hee - dle!
f
Well, all
pp
E9
f
Well, all right then, cats!
A6
Well,
right then, cats!
(claps)
Yes, yes, Ba - by, I know
f
RUTH: (in a trance)
pp
D9
yes, yes, Ba - by, I know That old man Mose Kicked the
sub. pp

D9
A6
buck - et, The old oak - en buck - et that hung in the well, Well,
well, well, Ba - by, I know No, no, was it red? No, no,
D9
no! Was it green, green, green is the col - or of my true love's hair,
A6
E9
Hair - breadth Har - ry with the floy, floy doy, floy doy, floy doy, floy
(sempre pp)

(Shout)
mp, (lyrically)
A6
doy, hoy! Hoy dre(h)eamt hoy dwe(h)elt in ma(h)r - ble
(pp)
cresc. poco a poco
halls well_ that ends well,_ well, well, Ba - by I know___ No,
cresc. poco a poco
D9
no, Was it green? No, no, no, Was it red sails in the sun - set call - in'
A6
me, me,_ me.___ You good for noth - in' Mi - mi, mi - mi,

RUTH: E9
f
dim.
Me Tar - zan, You Jane, Swing - in' in the trees, Swing - in' in the
CHORUS:
f
Tch
f
dim.
trees, Swing - in' in the trees, Swing-in', Swing-in',
p
mf
mp
p
tch tch tch tch
p
Swing - in', Swing - in', Swing- in', Swing - in',
più dim.
tch tch tch tch
più dim.

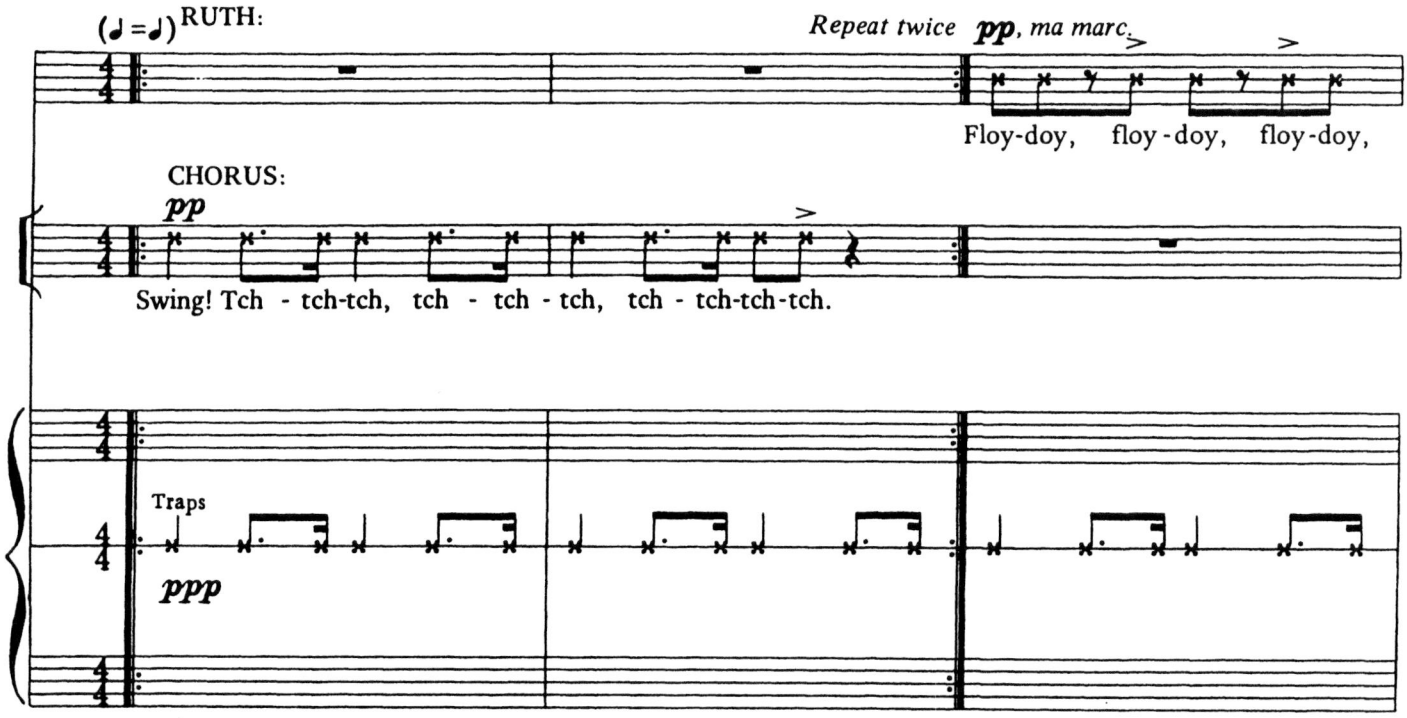
(♩=♩) RUTH:
Repeat twice pp, ma marc.
Floy-doy, floy-doy, floy-doy,
CHORUS:
pp
Swing! Tch - tch-tch, tch - tch - tch, tch - tch-tch-tch.
Traps
ppp

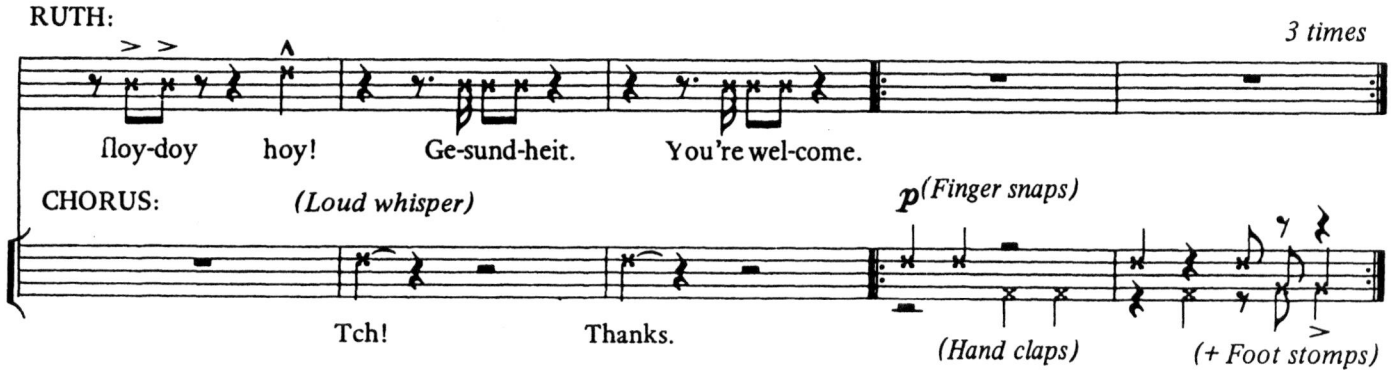
RUTH:
3 times
floy-doy hoy! Ge-sund-heit. You're wel-come.
CHORUS:
(Loud whisper)
p (Finger snaps)
Tch! Thanks.
(Hand claps)
(+ Foot stomps)

f
p
(snap)
(clap clap)
(snap)
(claps)
Whoa! Come on, Jack-son, You're get - ting hep.

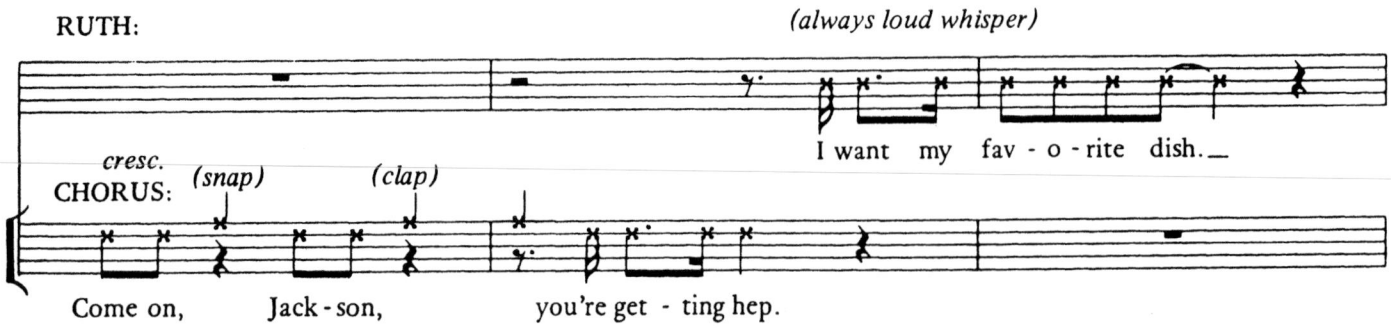
RUTH:
(always loud whisper)
I want my fav - o - rite dish.
cresc.
CHORUS:
(snap)
(clap)
Come on, Jack - son, you're get - ting hep.

RUTH:
3 times
Ge-sund-heit.
It's noth-ing.
CHORUS:
(Tongue clicks)
Whistle:
Fish.
Thanks.
(Click, clock, click, clock, click, clock) (Whoo!)

CHORUS:
(clap)
(They snap on off-beats)
Sol - id, groov-y, jiv - y, sound of swing!
Tch -
p

FIRST MAN:
swing!
Ah, do it!
[Speedy V. on clarinet]
8
mp
cresc.

SECOND MAN: FIRST GIRL:

Sol - id, Jack-son! Sea - food, Ma - ma

mf

il basso marcato

SECOND GIRL:

(A long banshee wail)

cresc.

f

TUTTI: *f*

Go! Go! Go! Go!

f sempre

Yah!

cresc.

Sol - id!
più f cresc.
TUTTI: ff
Swing!
Swing!
Oh,
ff
swing it!
marc.
cresc.
3
fff

RUTH: *(alone)(in a hoarse, hypnotic whisper)*

RUTH:
Down in the well, well, well, well My fa - vor-ite dish Ahh fish!
CHORUS:
[From offstage]
Ge -
(Her hands before her, mesmerized.)
[Exit.]
Thank you.
Swing, swing, swing, swing,
(sempre dim.)
sund-heit.
You're wel-come.
Swing, swing, swing, swing,
sempre dim.
swing, swing!
swing, swing!
3
ff sub.
gliss.
gliss.
sf
fff
long
sffz

It's Love

Lyrics by
BETTY COMDEN and ADOLPH GREEN

Eileen, Baker and Chorus

Music by
LEONARD BERNSTEIN

Copyright © 1953 by Amberson Holdings LLC, Betty Comden and Adolph Green
Copyright Renewed
Chappell & Co. and Leonard Bernstein Music Publishing Company LLC, Publishers
Copyright For All Countries All Rights Reserved

Bm7/A
D9 D
EILEEN:
Em
cresc.
B7
Em
G7/D
You're a sil - ly boy. You're in love with Ruth.
cresc.
G7
f
C
Am7
Dm7sus
Em/G
It's love! It's love! Come on now, Just try it.
mf
Dm7 Em7
C6
A7
EILEEN:
f
Dm7
G7
BAKER: (hesitatingly)
p
Don't try to de - ny it,
It's love! It's love!
p

Dm7
G7
Am
Am7/G
D7
I know the signs, I know it when I see it,
f

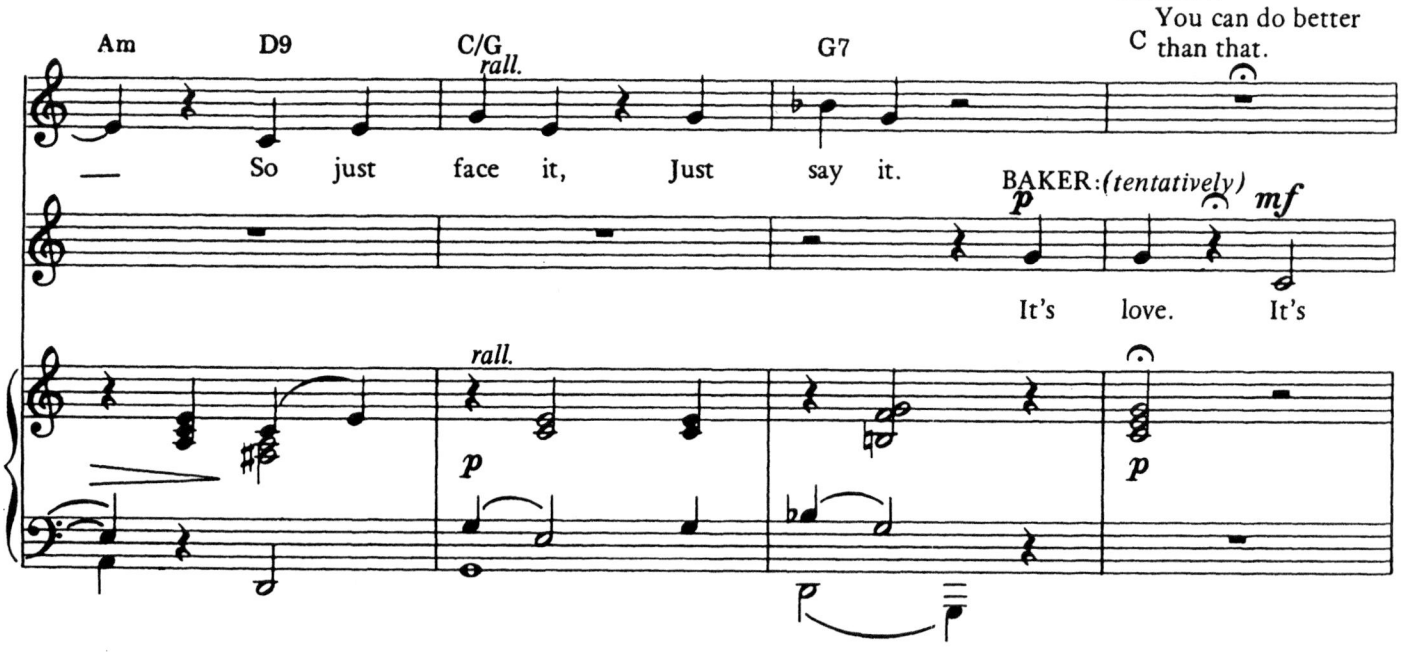
Am
D9
C/G
rall.
G7
C
EILEEN:
You can do better than that.
So just face it, Just say it.
BAKER: (tentatively)
p
mf
It's love. It's
rall.
p
p

F
EILEEN:
Try again!
A7
EILEEN:
See you later. (Exit)
Am9
ff
p
love! It's love!
May - be, It's
mf
fz
ff
p

Dmaj7
(With motion)
cresc. poco a poco (gaining conviction)
Bm7
Em7
A7
Em
A7
mf
love! It's love! Well, who would have thought it! If
p
cresc.
mf
D6
B7
Em7
A7
Em7
A7
mp
this is love, Then why have I fought it? What a
p
Bm
E9
E6
E9
Bm
E6
E9
way to feel! I could touch the sky. What a
F♯m
C♯7
C♯9
F♯m
f
A11
f
Dmaj7
cresc.
way to feel, I'm a dif-f'rent guy! It's love! At
cresc.
f

Bm7
Em7
A7
Em
A7
D6
B7
last, I've some-one to cheer for! It's love, At last, I've
Em7
A7
A9
Bm
Bm7/A
learned what we're here for. I've heard it said: "You'll
mf
espressivo
Bm6
broadly
E9
D
rall.
A7
know it when you see it." Well, I see it, I know it, It's
broadly
f
rall.
Dmaj7
BAKER:
Bm7
Em7
A7
Em
A7
love! La da dee da da da
CHORUS:
f
It's love! Well, who would have thought it! If
f

D6 B7 Em7 C A7 Em7 A7
love! La da dee da da da What a
this is love, Then why have I fought it? What a
p
Bm E9 E6 E9 Bm E6 E9 F#m
way to feel! I could touch the sky. What a way to
way to feel! I could touch the sky. What a way to
C#7 C#9 Solo: F#m A11 Dmaj7 Bm7
feel, I'm a dif-f'rent guy! It's love! At last, I've
feel. It's love! At last, I've
f

Em7
A7
Em
A7
D6
B7
some-one to cheer for! It's love! At last, I've
some-one to cheer for! It's love! At last, I've
Em7
A7
A9
Solo:
Bm
Bm7/A
learned what we're here for. I've heard it said: "You'll
learned what we're here for.
mf
espressivo
Bm6
broadly
E9
D/A
rall.
A7
Tutti:
Maestoso
D6
know it when you see it." Well, I see it, I know it, It's love!
Maestoso
broadly
rall.
ff

The Wrong Note Rag

Ruth, Eileen and Chorus

Lyrics by
BETTY COMDEN
and ADOLPH GREEN

Music by
LEONARD BERNSTEIN

Copyright © 1953 by Amberson Holdings LLC, Betty Comden and Adolph Green
Copyright Renewed
Chappell & Co. and Leonard Bernstein Music Publishing Company LLC, Publishers
Copyright For All Countries All Rights Reserved

B♭
B
mp
the town,_ sweep - in' the town.
Doo
sfz
mp
E
B7aug5
doo doo doo doo doo doo doo doo doo___ doo doo___
E
___ doo doo doo doo___ doo doo___ doo Doo doo doo Doo doo doo doo
B7aug5
cresc.
f B7
E F7
unis.
p
doo doo doo___ They call___ it the Wrong Note Rag! It's
cresc.
f
sfz
p

B♭
F7
got a lit - tle twist that sim - ply drives you in - sane, drives you
in - sane, drives you in - sane, drives you in - sane. Be -
B♭
F7
cause you find you nev - er get it out of your brain, out of
your brain, out of your brain!
B♭
B
mp
Doo
sfz
mp

E
B7aug5
doo doo doo doo doo doo doo doo doo doo doo
E
doo doo doo doo doo doo doo Doo doo doo doo doo doo doo
B7aug5
cresc.
B7
E
F7
doo doo doo They call it the Wrong Note Rag!
cresc.
f
sfz
gliss.
CHORUS:
ff C
F
F♯7/E
B/D♯
B
Bun-ny Hug! Tur-key Trot! Gim-me the Wrong Note Rag!
ff

* Ruth may sing one octave lower.

* These four bars may be shouted.

[Piano Solo]
ff
First time: Trumpets play
Second time: CHORUS sings
ff
Doo
(loco both times)
sffz
ff
doo doo doo doo doo doo doo doo doo doo doo doo doo doo doo doo
doo doo doo doo doo doo doo doo doo doo doo doo They call

1st time: CHORUS:
2nd time: Trumpets
___ it the Wrong Note Rag! trem. Doo doo doo doo doo doo doo
(2nd time 8va)
sffz
doo doo doo___ doo doo___ doo doo doo doo___ doo doo___ doo doo
doo doo doo doo doo doo doo doo doo___ They call___ it the Wrong Note Rag!
1.
2.
Rag!
Tutti
Yeah!
sffz ff